MYSELF AND OTHER STRANGERS

ROBIN LINDSAY WILSON

INDEPENDENT INNOVATIVE INTERNATIONAL

Published by Cinnamon Press
Meirion House
Tanygrisiau
Blaenau Ffestiniog
Gwynedd, LL41 3SU
www.cinnamonpress.com

The right of Robin Lindsay Wilson to be identified as author of this work has been asserted by him in accordance with the Copyright, Designs and Patent Act, 1988. Copyright © 2015 Robin Lindsay Wilson
ISBN: 978-1-909077-83-6
British Library Cataloguing in Publication Data. A CIP record for this book can be obtained from the British Library.

Designed and typeset in Palatino by Cinnamon Press. Printed in Poland

Cover design by Adam Craig from original artwork 'The Puppets are Waiting — Charlie' by Alice McMurrough, sued with kind permission.

Cinnamon Press is represented in the UK by Inpress Ltd www.inpressbooks.co.uk and in Wales by the Welsh Books Council www.cllc.org.uk

Acknowledgements

Thanks to the editors who have published poems appearing in this collection: Natural Patterns – published in *Brittle Star* Issue 21; Ayrshire Geometry – published *Chapman* No 83; Growing Up In A Dinghy – published in *Poetry Monthly* Issue 144; The Beautiful Game – published in *Brittle Star* Issue 21; Growing Up In A Free Market Economy – published in *Envoi* Issue 155; My Amazing Shrinking Friend – published in *Poetic Licence* Issue 30; Inheritance – published in *Envoi* Issue 160; Vocation – published in *Magma* Issue 55; My Life From Very Far Away – published in *Rain Dog* Issue 13; Weapons of Modesty – published in *Never Bury Poetry* Issue 64; Vanity and Progress – published in *The Journal* Issue 33; The Effect of Clean Sheets on Monsters – published in *The Journal* Issue 11; Nemesis – published in *The Journal* Issue 11; Arm – published *The Journal* Issue 15; Finding the Quarry – published in *The Journal* Issue 18; Pilgrims Returning Home – published in *Other Poetry* Series III No. 3; Jackson Pollock's Pizza Bar – published in *The Journal* Issue 27; Songs of Experience – published in *Envoi* Issue 164; Lion Dance – published in *Decanto* Issue 19; The Threatened Bride – published in *The Interpreter's House* Issue 41; Beasts – published in *Other Poetry* Series 4, No. 7 (2012); Unfamiliar Territory – published in *Roundyhouse* Issue 21; Fallen – published in *The Eildon Tree* Issue 19/20; Post Coital Reverie – published in *Frogmore Papers* No. 73; Learning to Buy Flowers – published in *Bluechrome Anthology* 2004; Holding Flowers – published *Poetic Licence* 28 & *Eildon Tree* Issue 16; The Failure of Self Definition – published in *Decanto* Issue 12; Opposite of Freedom – published *Agenda*; Still Life – published by *Reach* Issue 127; Christmas Dinner – published in *The Journal* Issue 27; The Constant Husband – published in *The Journal* Issue 15; Arrezzo Bus – published in *Frogmore Papers* Issue 82; Skye Blues – published in *Iota* Issue 85; Grudge Match – published Frogmore Papers No.77; The Problem With Gifts – published *Brittle Star* Issue 21; The Cooling of Water – published in *Other Poetry* No. 32; Last Holiday at Balnakeil – published in *Current Accounts* Issue 29; Easter – published in *Other Poetry* Series 4 No. 5 (2012); Between Names – published in *Brittle Star*; Tree Theory – published in *The Journal* Issue 36; Opportunities Beyond the Garden – winner of Tenby Poetry Competition 2012

Contents

To John, Paul, George, Bob,
Lenny and Ringo
for making me listen.

To Susie

with Love.

Myself and Other Strangers

Castles

some words
sit on a rock
like Edinburgh Castle

tourists of higher ground
reach it with one breath

but I go around —
forget it's there
in the labyrinth of second hand
book shop bargains
until I listen to myself
saying anything to please

one day
I'm going to write down
an Edinburgh Castle
of a word

a word that keeps
its palace inside granite —
a word to quicken my breath
and give me sore legs

so that I cannot say
justice or *trust*
without hard work

Natural Patterns

he
climbs down
leaf after leaf
and surrounds
neglected water
with silver roots

the tree is a boy
with elm hands
ready to respond
to faint fossil edges
and giant patterns
of flooded memory

the tree laughs

it is a young man
returned handsome
from brighter trees
and harder water
to flotsam seams
left on pebbles
and the buried
long cold seeds
of his accent

the tree fades

it is an old man
with autumn arms
re-using light
and numb leaves
to build the future

completely happy
in the architecture
of his own country
he climbs back
into branches
and is home

Ayrshire Geometry

wee steeples
in raining green villages

wee steeples
for plain we people
never generous
or dark desperate
in their cul-de-sacs
to adorn a monument
with extravagant height
gargoyles
curving stone hosannas

short of heaven
this spurt of property
well below the hospital chimney

I look across
the horizontal bay
I'm 5 feet 8
and nothing I've wanted
has been as high
as a spire
raised by public subscription

nothing I've made
has been as proud
and modest
as Ayrshire geometry

Growing Up in a Dinghy

The boat changed its voice
as it entered shallow water.

The possibility of silence
fell upon us from the shore.
As the diesel engine idled
deep well-travelled voices
took their strange stories
from the marrow of my bones.

The two-stroke revved,
shuddered and lost pitch.

Whispers navigated the cove,
gravel welcomed the keel.
I was happy to go home
but longed for the vibration
of a story in open water.

The Beautiful Game

below the water tower
the rusting blaise pitch
was a Sunday on Mars
with goal posts each end

three-footballing boys
twisted tilted and dived
like faulty spaceships

a giant drum hovered
over tackles and saves

it's like a flying Saucer

said Donald Mitchell
— his McEwan's strip
was shrill and half lit

we could paint it
with flames blasting out
instead of concrete legs

the black tower leaned
over Jim playing keepie-up
tripping him from behind

how much for the paint?

Jason nodded for possession
dribbled across the park
and shot into an undefended
slab of oblong light

nothing like a UFO!

he booted the ball back
aimed it at the hut wall
and before the rebound
Donald's orbit decayed

Glasgow spun below him

blurring faster and wilder
with all its weekdays
feeling like crash landings
and a water tower shadow
over his filthy hangover

Growing Up in a Free Market Economy

Skeeter throws a softball
against the raw brick wall

the drugstore afternoon
grins him another freckle

you can be my best friend

he says when he kicks dust
into the middle of next week

the bright next-door boy
has never been restless —
he loves American trees

you can be my best friend

ball slow hup-thumping
against a chirping backyard

it's the end of the holidays
windy in the emptiest state —
it's the beginning of need

you can be my best friend

he says between knocks
of the side kicked ball
returned by his neighbour

he is waiting for an answer

throughout the heartland
happy goalmouths open
teachers' sad eyes open
fathers' grim mouths open

employers take him in
and the answer is a smile
for the very last time

My Amazing Shrinking Friend

I heard the pavement crack

privet hedges sang the blues —
limping dogs zigzagged
between deep throated tulips
and the off-license turned black

we loitered under nicotine flats
by defaced no loitering signs —
I tried to inhale a joint
and hold it in my blood

wanting appearance money
or a silver screen imagination
I hung loose in a doorway

listening to my best friend
empty lungs of grace notes
in a thankless one God town

I lied to make an ending
of adolescence and loyalty —
bored watching slow buses
and the universe expand

Inheritance

listen
fidgets of autumn leaves
fingering campus lawns

a season of hoping over

failed students re-sitting
their half-hearted summers
and losing sleep again

what do I know?
how do I change?

at the back of chapel
the freedom to disappoint
draws me like the smell
of decay in the soil

I could gather mushrooms
and the webs of leaves
for my father's offering

I study rashness in winter
and pornography in spring
I test my luck in silent bars
and between hangovers —
under the faintest stars
I learn the theory of everything

the disgrace of lethargy
requires less explanation
than the disgrace of stupidity
when I take my face home

Final Judgement

you blame english history
and the secret civil war
you say has never ended
for your lack of success

squinting at a class list
you're a revolutionary
on the first day of university
with a manifesto to sell
but no friends to radicalise

you blame volatile markets
you blame the new government
for a failure to connect
but you sometimes relax
and practice binge-drinking
when the CIA isn't looking

I do not blame you
for the slimy cat litter
or the avocado seeds
stuck with toothpicks
suspended over water

it's my fault somehow
I can see it in your eyes

blamed for wanting you —
destroying your control
by inventing a conspiracy
to love and be frivolous

I will stand with you
in the shabby garden
behind your tenement flat
and look up at windows
for evidence of surveillance
and then I will leave you

Vocation

At a black-grease factory,
with the weight of sleep
still clogging your veins,
you stumble clocking on.

While other boys wrestle
with a spark-limbed octopus
and turn their dreams to solder,
you unwind wood-shavings
to the source of pleasure.

Left alone you conjure
rinds of pine fragrance
from a piece of wood.

The market surges then dips,
until factories let men go.

But at your workstation,
under metal-framed windows,
a peel of honey-wood
snakes around your wrist.
And outside the compound
the dark horizon hardens
and unwinds a secret promise
from the most unlikely sky.

Bees

Parked beside the fruitbox trash
of Mr. Singh's corner-shop in Partick,
with the lorry shedding raindrops,
from juddering drop-down sides -
I'm flatfooted over shaking crates
of clinking glass-necked prisms
while sunlight brims the bottles
with a squirm of carbonated sugar.

I belong to a generation of creatures,
born to rummage and shuffle colour
through free-enterprise geometry
without the impulse of ambition.

I feel like a bee in cargo pants
clambering over a honeycomb
of volcanic Iron-Bru and Tizer
with only my muscles thinking.

The alternative is an army career
and humming over ammo-crates
in bigger boots and hotter weather.

I want home to a steeply sloping street
where rain falls to dull the possible.
I have no business being brightly lit
by the hiss of sweetened chemicals
or the glare of deserts and battle.

My Life from Very Far Away

the orbit I made
around your party
was inspired
by doubt and vodka

a single strand
of porch light
or woman's laughter
kept me bound

my evening trail
was a flimsy lie
staggering to a tune
of gravel paths
bedding plants
monochrome grass
tea-lights in trees
stars and jealousy

the orbit I made
beyond your guests
was a reflex action
an endless wobble
— distracted motion
wishing to love

after the party
I had four ideas
written on my hand

two were indecent
one was cruel
and the last idea
I cut with thorns

I was so proud

Weapons of Modesty
for Gwen John

the brown between
this room brown
and set brown lips
is nothing you can see

all these browns
fell on my imagination
and I did not blink

I thought one dull thought
started one dull action
endured in a different brown
wanted in a different brown

I sat perfectly still
you did not take my hand

I was silent
but you did not ask me
to break your heart

if I smile
the Gods will be jealous

my dress is brown
to avoid their punishment

my work is brown
to test your sensitivity

and if I die
without your attention
I will know
I got the better of you

because changing colours
was your responsibility

Alternative Potential

black heap in a gold clearing

it's winter smouldering in reverse
raising small orange suns
from the dead souls of leaves

it's windfall sycamore
horse-chestnut and oak this time —
something more personal
leaking rot underneath

a smell like the fast release
of Wellingtons or an early
discovery of damp groin
makes you sorry for people
you do not want to know

you feel like lying naked
under slimy black leaves
being smothered by winter

in the unimpressed distance
there's a nation of trees
or thoughts or dark skin

it's too far to be certain
all the branches look the same

but with a change of wind
the sorrow will leave you

you will want to see it burn

Vanity and Progress

while the tiny fires
started by his halo
spread into the park
the matchhead man
is dreaming of war

the rained on crowd
gather around his idea
of splitting obligations
relationships and atoms
with a simple bonfire

the sea and sky burn
taking faith with them

the switches behind
his rubbed red eyes
are permanently on

no more darkness
due to his imagination

napalm and semtex
on portable screens
and you with a fuse
ready for the next world

we disperse the night
taking the park with us
on phones and cameras

we grow granules
of pretty dark-matter
in unforgiving eyes

your feeling of revenge
is the least of our worries

The Effect of Clean Sheets on Monsters

death squad mercenaries
torturers child-porn film makers
school boys with blood
sprayed across their faces

sleep on fresh pillows

acid bath butchers pimps
sweat-shop slave masters
arms dealers assassins
sister fucking adulterers

dip their delicate feet
into a tucked cotton wave

their bad lives are good
while there's a virgin edge
to unpick with sweating toes

when dictators rapists terrorists
ethnic cleansing architects
are served with clean sheets

their hairy legs scissor out
as innocent sleepy visitors
rewarding a day's labour
with the forever touch
of a lovely ironed corner
never conquered before

murderers have hard knees
that search silent sheets
for cool honest opposition
to rest their fever upon

Nemesis

I burn barns
I poison wells

This is not a mask

I pilot planes
into office towers

The face you see now
is the face you changed
the first time
I saw you kiss
another man

I post anthrax letters
I explode smallpox bombs

This is not a mask

This is the face
you changed
when you denied my name

I am coming
to your home town
with explosives
around my waist

This is not my face
this is the whirlwind
you set free
when you broke my faith
broke my dignity

I grow mushroom clouds
in suitcases
because you do not love me

I am coming
with bare teeth
and bare hands
because I had a face
and you looked away

Arm

I'm a battle blackened soldier
but this flesh between my face
and the temple is pillow clean.

The jungle stinks of armpits.

I can hear the fallen gibbons
screaming for their leaves again.

This unseasoned arm is shelter
retrieved from the litter of war.
The only piece still innocent
to open a lover's mouth upon.

One arm on which to shake and hope.

Finding the Quarry

escaping the scene of the crime
you find an unhurried atrocity

plane trees lapping the gully
a window shutter springing open

machete screams behind the maize

a dust-devil of temptation spirals
across stubble cleared ground
and trips under your horse's hooves

the cicadas stop for no reason
— the silence has no patience

to slip reason as simply as a latch?
to trust conscience to the wind?

the dust-devil does not reappear

the same shutter bangs closed
then the cicadas speak to you

you turn your horse to the path

nothing makes it your business

The Power of Advertising

her huge sweaty breasts
blockade the balcony
and threaten to eclipse
the town's only statue

reinforcing rods poke
beyond a plaster hand
of rain softened fingernails
that drip drip drip

the soldier is pockmarked
where bullets impacted —
his whip has crumbled —
a wire holds the centre
as tiny rosettes of cement
swing in a shore breeze

it cannot be determined
if the man is about to strike
or rush to lift the cross
from this fallen Christ

curling through dirty gaps
in the irreducible scuffle
of Jesus and his burden
the tomato plants refuse
to keep their edges green

in the city centre flats
a woman calculates tax
against her husband's overtime

her calyx nipples blush
and feel like motherhood
pressed against the stucco
as she tries to catch sight
of the Firestone factory gates
behind his crown of thorns

Pilgrims Returning Home

the safe route disappears
but no one asks to get off

darkness dissolves the driver
who steers with eyes closed —
letting his forearms guess

the man in the back seat
has no reason to go home —
the girl beside him is a bore
boasting of a pretty address

a punk learning French
re-reads the same sentence
then travels without verbs —
head back and mouth slack

each woman turns to stone
each man turns to bronze
behind noisy black windows
the passengers go to hell

they hold no regret or fear
when the bus tilts forwards
and smoking wheels descend

the punk finishes his book
the back seat man laughs
at the rich girl's bad joke
puts a hand on the buzzer

Lost and Open

a high monoblock wall
in an unfamiliar part of town
refuses to be a metaphor

this is a day of pigeons
on cracked pavements

the sky over nurses' flats
is the only blue I can see

debris of minor pleasures
litter the unpleasant lawn
and I become selfless here

if you dismiss your shade
or you walk towards me
I will give myself to you

there's too much wall
nothing advances to begin
nothing recedes to end
guilt initiates no rhythm

I could take out my wallet
keep the untroubled money
put the rest in a letter box
if there was a letter box here

be blank in a blank town
free to abandon belonging

I could break to be kind
I could interrupt to be good

or praise the loveless past
or want your grassy arms
all the way around me

no windfall luck today
while I look for a new name

my best rituals are profane
my family's gift is sabotage

and the same day travels
with me while I murder
all the things I could be

Jackson Pollock's Pizza Bar

now there's no clear narrative
just market forces and greed
and no pretence of history —
beginnings middles and ends

just one rudimentary meal
eaten from a cardboard box
on an imitation marble table
with a plastic cup of froth

crumbs and polish beneath
splats of colored polymers —
fractals in a cheap universe
of how you feel right now

only snatched gratification
a reward for helplessness

your hunger after my hunger
looking for an end to want
in a menu of pizza toppings

because patterns look familiar
does not make them relevant
or give your life a story

Songs of Experience

the pattern I make inside myself
and the pattern I make Tuesday
on the pad beside the telephone
change the pattern of the future

here's a pattern unzipping its flies

here's a tiny pattern coming back
in a big self addressed envelope

my odd little soul does not insist
on the one true pattern of God
it likes to wander into eddies
and flurries of haphazard deities
until it is claimed by beauty

here's a nasty drunken pattern
promising a clear sky to a child

here's a pattern I caught in my sleep
because I was afraid of waking

my soul returns to the first pattern —
the hurt songs my father sang
and I sing them again for him

creation sings patterns of its own

the song I make in the shower
changes the pattern of my belief

Lion Dance

he stepped out of a girlfriend

the room had neat spaces
celebrating its anniversary

he wanted to meet a lioness
and a mirror to be strange in

but he saw her perfect legs
naked in high heels
next to his favourite song

he saw her brief bad hair
under a blond chandelier
surrounded by intellectual women
with hours of expensive lotion
on their hungry shoulders

she said she'd never met a lion

he said he knew a foreign zoo
where they could elope

she stepped into his roar
and the bars disappeared
in front of them both

The Threatened Bride

Thieves broke into Gustav Klimt's studio but left his painting
'The Bride' untouched on its easel.

the tall thief wanted jewellery
when he splintered the door
but when he found costumes
from the ballet and the opera
he hoisted a damp pink boa
and staggered to its magic

the short thief spat loudly
and searched for gold leaf

the bride hid in moonlight
but her back was an easel
easily kicked down

the squat man hid his face
he had never been a groom
or seen a woman naked

the tall man drew his knife
wanting to make her bleed
but did not touch her skin

she accused with pubic hair
and the musk of love-making
opening her legs to them

the thieves retraced their steps
silent all the way home

the tall man fathered sons —
the squat man married twice
but the ghost of pleasure
haunted them each night
and never let them rest

Beasts

while throwing a hoop
over by the clown heads
you hear a canine snarl
and the grunt of an inquiry

she laughs at your gift
of a goldfish and a toy
but you feel luck has arrived
with the kiss of a free throw

her voice echoes low -
makes a new emotion
of your over polite reply

like a scabby dog shaking —
spiraling water-drops
against a sudden hurt -
she's inside your chest

then she's bursting balloons
with hidden black claws
and blowing you a kiss
with her tongue exposed

you stare right back
at her pimpled flesh —
she plays a princess
waiting for you to beg

you break eye contact —
she spits a mongrel curse
and straddles a dodgem
on its way to a collision

now you have no dignity
or any scent to confess
you sink into the sawdust
and howl howl howl
howl howl with relief

Camposanto Apocalypse

devils bubble off the plaster
spitting fire at the illiterate —
stabbing fins into the poor
until only justice remains

at the end of all our days
I am naked in that crowd
with green scales on my tail
remembering the first sins
of deception and exposure
petty jealousy and shame
that gathered random cells
and grew hunger into fangs

there is no edge of shadow
to locate the place or time
when flesh hardened to horn —
everything is electric light
and an evening with friends
when fingers curl into claws

I growl to defend a wife —
I thicken with rind and fat
to distract myself from care

while my eyes catch fire
I trade gifts with the world
and break them on my sons

their puffy children's fists
pull down my shouting voice
until truth is neither cloven foot
nor a downy angel's wing

here beside the Field of Miracles
there is only transformation
and the most humdrum terror
in the hearts of angry families
studying filaments of damp

I no longer recognise myself
nor hope to do a good turn —
all I have is appetite

Moving as an Animal

I was a flock of borrowed feathers
rushing white-washed walls
trying to find an open window
when you picked me for the dance

I was a local plague of magpies
stealing all the best mornings
when you borrowed my pen
with its ink of grey harvests

I was an evening of mobbing crows
flapping in the wrong direction
when you asked for a drink
and I teetered with a party-tray

I moved like a new creature
with simple thoughts in its fins
when you returned from holiday
and financed new friends

from second to second
I am the first feathered bird
thinking its wings control
white high-sided clouds

brilliant with every move
when you fall to kiss me

The History of Energy

I wanted to climb the river
I conquered as a slippery boy —
she wanted to dwindle

I wanted to feel the wind
putting muscles in my limbs —
she wanted to eat chocolate

I started shallow and slow
but the sun turned green
and the river was willing

I was over black-heart water
released ahead of my feet
invisible with manoeuvring
from devil-rock god-rock
to god-rock devil-rock

the monster rising up

I spun around teetering
and ran back civilised
to her wool slumped body

she might start travelling
with a river in that car

I can take it with me
this good and strange
careless river manhood
climbing married lives
of history and future now

if she climbs with me

Fallen

sunlight unbalanced us —
we fell onto pink petals
and freshly mown grass

grubby blossoms hid
the nape of your neck
and filled dark contours
of elbows and shins

our smiles converged —
meaning was bewildered
by colour and memory
but comfort remained

only one breath ruffled
the speckled garland
between your nose
and my parted lips

no judgement stirred
behind unblinking eyes
until insects found us

when ants scrabbled
over our folded bodies
and stole the flowers
between our thighs
we returned to light

with every petal gone
the grain of our bones
served other seasons —
but this is the memory
of how my itch began

Unfamiliar Territory

we make no sense
with a wide-angle lens
of intermittent hills
or floating sunlight

I catch you shouting
as the shadows pass —
we're quieter under blue
but we do not relax

there's nothing else to do
with unfamiliar territory
except record we are here
this time in a safer car

we continue whispering
in different clothes —
careful in this situation
of how we pronounce
the names of hills

let's go
before the sky breathes out
we do not need a camera
if the place is small

let's go
to a wordless bed
with little defense
against the soulful sweep
of acid wasted rocks
and northern disappointment

let's go
and be intimate forever

Post-coital Reverie

his mouth breathed in the hair
disappearing behind her ear
towards sleep and perfume

he kissed her lips greedily -
mouth breaking her schemes

she was loved in filthy cinemas
and for a long time after loving
he talked her into trusting him

she felt certain of pleasure
thinking of him walking home
under fruit trees near a hungry river

she was full of his enthusiasm
when she had a white silk skirt
and three obliging silk men
introducing her to the next craze

it's a sports car indulgence
to wear her silly hair undone

her open blouse is a conversation
between her need to be lost
and her desire to remain

because he is under a pergola
promising clematis and wisteria
does not mean she will return

or that her love of being in love
was the most romantic thing
that ever happened to him

Learning to Buy Flowers

there's a sensitive frost
across the football pitch

I stop in my tracks
gaze back at my footprints
and wonder what I'll miss

it's not the southlight
honeying our front room
it's your occasional extravagant
vase of sprawling flowers

pollen and warm petals
on the spring time table

fresh cut carnations
are birthday presents –
an infrequent dinner guest
and last minute smartening up

but the lily breaking open —
the poppy heart exploding
during all those shut off
shrugged off declining days
is comfortable splendour

and if I had to leave you
I would always remember
falling tulips and daffodils
lighting the cup of the afternoon

and with all the leaving done
I would buy a bunch of flowers

Holding Flowers

Women hug -
Close like a child
— Creamy lilies
Stroking mouth skin

Like caressing
A baby's head

With men it's distance —
They need objectivity

In case the bouquet
Turns them into fools —
The gift too obvious
To hide rejection

What a weak man
What a soft mark
You can cheat him

Betray his passion
With a simple smile
Or a giggle of petals

Men know love
Eats their pride

Safer to hold flowers
Away from the heart

Failure of Self Definition

from bowling club railings
I throw myself into traffic
for something young to do

I want to loiter with intent
under your Habitat blinds
or your thick trained hedge

but I haven't got the voice
to sing you a love song

I want to smell the sweat
on your summer garden
while you push me around
in a beat up wheelbarrow

I want to damage your car
with dope smoke and burns —
a couple of handbrake turns
and hot fog on the windows

but I haven't got the brains
to buy a bunch of flowers

the bowling club railings
sing convincing midnights
from another boy's sky

but I can never be spontaneous
— someone might get hurt

The Opposite of Freedom

the dark things you coaxed from the earth
and instructed to impede my journey
rose against my charms and settled will —
keeping my bones pressed to the mattress
and my work diverted by an Ansaphone

the soft things you combed from clouds
and shredded through the tops of trees
until they hated the light they came from
fell upon my negotiation of city corners
and returned me to my childhood fears

the cold things you clawed from the ocean
slithered into my favourite search-engine
to short-circuit power-point presentations
and mock every connection to promotion
until my password was returned unknown

and now I don't do anything but sleep —
I don't do anything but repeat accusations
into potted plants and dead white-goods

I will open a bottle of Baillie Nicol Jarvie —
close the window shutters and lock the door
in case you find the power to destroy dreams

Still Life

for Georges Braque

reviewing my table top
you judge a quite life

the evidence is silent —
a morning paper safe
under the coffee-mill

but between the guitar
and the fruit bowl
many good friends
rose and fell beside me

it takes a million ideas
to plunge the cafetière
or fold the front page

did you see us dance
among broken crockery
regretting the dawn
and making promises?

the stained tablecloth
was soaked in bleach
half squashed plantains
were hastily replaced —
blood wiped from cruets

I am ready to start again

the belle epoch is here
beginning in this room

one eternal moment
between my wife's hand
and the butter knife

Christmas Dinner

one lanky carrot chopped
and the hostess is tempted
to slaughter her family

her girl's planning to get fat
her boy's studying to be a cat —
both whispering under the table
flirting with harm's way

her best saucepan burns
fat spits at the wet sink
— she sluices ectoplasm
and rubs ghostly trails
of fragrant goose grease
into scalding clean water

there was one Christmas
as a proper little madam —
Christmas as a champion
and Christmas in her own place
— that Christmas in control

the embarrassed guest
stands in the doorway
with mistletoe in hand

The Constant Husband

for Clare & Charlie

the firefly crawled over him
but he could not see its light
he was looking for his wife
in the moon stunned barley fields

the insect hung inside his jacket
but he did not see it glow
he was searching for his wife
among the staring sunflower heads
and between the barks of dogs

on the side of the suitcase
bumping off his right leg
the firefly danced for itself

but he did not see it flicker
he was listening to the stream
saying this is where she is

she opened the green door
to the spilling midnight pool

he took off his clothes

the firefly burned the water dry
and shone upon their only bed
with longing without shadow
and all the faith of his journey

Arrezzo Bus

the Italian sun
has a left arm
to stroke lovers
and a strong right
to punch priests

it has a pink robe
to empty distance
on the horizon
and make it plenty

by the harbour
and the breakwater
the mother's blue
never needs mending

the sun has a lap
with a hive of light
squirming over knees —
it feels like adoration

and here we are
in our little white bus
spiralling the dust
of dead sunflowers
and olive fields
beyond the possibility
of a goodbye

David
Benedict
Clare

we have a left arm
for remembering —
a tanned right arm
for reaching

we touch brightness
as it breezes past

ambidextrous now
and never going home

Couch Potato
for Alison

in the winter
we look at our feet
in case they make us fall

in the summer
it is too hot
to go on holiday
so we plan it all
on paper scraps
weekends squander

in the spring
just the thought
of what we have to do
bolts the front door
and draws the curtains

this nest is temporary
we will make another
and take it with us —
it will be there
when we stop laughing

forgive what happens next
if you love me

my darling
in a couple of weeks —
in five years —
any second now
we will enter
our imagined lives

and if we do not wake up
we will still be in love

and if we have been asleep
for all these years
tonight we will embrace
and start dreaming again

The Origin of Movement

when did you giggle-listen —
lost to the cheering crowd
in the river's little wound?

when did the breeze bend
you across silver boughs
to whisper 'this is living?'

your shape over hot sand
once tall shadow rippled
and tip-toed to an ocean

a muscle made you laugh
each ball-and-socket joint
gifted a lifetime of friends

there was a simple hinge
swinging you into my days
where our marriage began

now your reflex is gravity
you need my full embrace
to lift you into memory

Skye Blues

the constellation of Mallaig
turns on its harbour lights
and sends silver filaments
across the Christmas water
like lost strands of lametta

the Ardvasar Hotel gives up
its obligation to celebrate

brown untidy bungalows
provide a kitsch spectacle
of bruised plastic snowmen
and sparkle-eyed reindeer
leaping electric blue icicles

dwarfs climb a snow-ladder
looking whisky malicious
and ready to snatch back
any gift Santa might offload

we're a couple of silhouettes
in front of a neon sleigh
warming ourselves on disdain

our New Year was a duty
and we are tired of caring

sorry for our bad temper
and what we failed to do
until the night hushes us
with an abracadabra of stars

Grudge Match

the old couple's chintz house
was split down the middle
for the audience to look in
and judge who was honest

deprived of convenience food
and integrated technology
the straight-backed woman
and the pipe smoking man
continued descending stairs
pulling out dangerous plugs
— waiting for a thunderbolt
or an uncontested memory

musty silences were filled
by ancient tissue ripping —
setting where the eyes set
behind the arthritic plot
of vindication and revenge

they coughed and rose again
after the crush-bar interval

both knew the secret law
of losing everyday things
to claim they were stolen
by a vindictive poltergeist
or a petty-minded spouse

after they took their bows
and left the provincial tour
both actors returned home
to the same mistakes again

The Problem with Gifts

music study thinned your hair
talent made you truculent —
my arm around your shoulder
withers as we stand here

there's less excuse for me
except a fashion for pale
that faded several years ago
and left me half invisible

the gifts we've discarded
decorate the kitchen walls —
there's your cello case
there's my little pottery jug

we only have each other now

I look like a fat clay pot —
you're as thin as a cello bow

neither gift uses the other

Imitations of Winter

Say something warming
but wait for my answer
because it's deep winter
and cold confounds us all.

Cloud the windscreen
with sighs and diplomacy
if you can't make a promise.
Imitate the winter howl,
make a ghostly noise
and keep me company.

I'd like a quick keepsake
of you confronting snow.
I'll stop on the hard-shoulder
at the emergency phone
for a zoom and a click.

You make me laugh
as flakes hit your tongue
with cross-eyed crazy stuff.
You mock swallow
the bad things of the past
as if snow was a remedy.

Behind you the trash
of a snow-plough ridge
melting in transparent curves
like broken specimen jars.

Winter is my passenger,
it gusts back swearing
and slams the car door.

Your silence is a highway
to the rest of the world.
My silence is cold bone
and a decision taken.

Expecting your love
is like asking the winter
to imitate the spring.

My smile kills winter.
Winter does not kill everything.

The Cooling of Water

afternoon departure
in a woman's rush

I sneer at the weight
and carry both cases

we wait for a taxi
without eye contact

I see her smile
only when she's gone

two floors above
I return to windows
and warm patches

the bathroom drips
smugness and vitality

there's a perfect bubble
on the shampoo bottle
— a curl of honey soap
leprous in its dish

her actions condense
on a shower screen

moisture shines
on vinyl walls —
jitterbugs farewell

the shower curtain
grows a bacillus —
it caught the spores
by falling in love
with a plastic bath

its kiss drying
is the sagging pace
of parting and loss

Last Holiday at Balnakeil

The sky ripped off its hinges.
Our whole breath went with it.

Both lifted for one heartbeat
until the sea breathed for us.

We floated over waves skilled
at suggesting a slow goodbye,
hoping for less responsibility
than sun-spray or salty cloud.

We blew kisses to your mother.

Her fragile shadow hunched
over two incendiary rocks.
You thought her face sank,
blind in bewilderment and fear.
I thought she was happy to go
where the tide dazzled her.

And the sky returned endless
from its holiday over icebergs
with a hundred more years
for us to investigate melting
and study migrating stones —
things of future significance.

But we would do these things alone.

Easter

your face is a cocoon
with a grub inside

thick spun in winter
the light in your skin
protects the idea within

but in spring
behind your eyes
a doppelganger
stirs involuntarily
and becomes conscious

the maggot eats
tissue and protein
until your face is tight
and every compromise
that pulled it slack
is rasped clean

who are you now?
what have you done
with your old life?

as days lengthen
the worm darkens

the facts you know
about adult identity
peel away and curl
like a discarded blister

let your soul emerge —
stretch its tender legs —
unfold iridescent wings
and catch the breeze

Between Names

I am half way home
in a second-hand hat
and widow's weeds,
feeling for a memory
between the bus stop,
brightening low cloud
and New Town breeze.

The estate is raw grass,
tearaways, mattresses
and pit-bull excrement.
Three concrete pipes
bury a roadside initiative
of mixed nursery trees.

That used to be farmland,
now it's Loch Etive Lane.
All I see are gravel chips
in fenceless driveways
and empty bird feeders
on trees from Japan.

I don't know who I am.

Once I had a maiden name —
once I had a Christian name —
once I had three children.

Now adolescent girls
hang upside down,
on a climbing-frame,
and spit at the burnt seat
on a wrecked seesaw.

I have no memory
of mountains or lochs
or why I married you.

When you are not here
each direction is the same.

Tree Theory

from the centre of the park
the tree breaks dark apart
and wind-flicks the particles
until some light falls out
onto a cocoon of scarves
cable-stitching breath

the red underside of leaves
crawls with bug geometry —
over the melted silver bark
summer never quite goes out

delinquent branches steal
sunshine from the breeze
and fumble tiny pleasures
of warmth and ruby colour
onto the federation of edges

richer than the autumn silt
travelling through its sap
the trunk hugs an empire
of fluctuations and alliances
beyond any crisis of death
or the rude transformation
of a sleepy season reversed

this dark maple flourishes
despite perpetual conspiracies
of jaws and wings and larvae —
it makes hope from changes

Opportunities Beyond the Garden

it's different from your wall
window and the cushion
under which you keep pain

it's mine with a garden

off the straight dirt path
I feel normal next to irises -
I'm happy turning sideways
and changing distances
because of rhododendrons

there's beech hedge wealth
between scratching home
and trampled barbed-wire

there's order between radishes
and yellow potato flowers

a twisted bramble head
crying for the sheltered side
between two tortured sheds
is squatting in the shadow
by the honest bracken

take shadows from me

in middling bungalow life
strike me if I'm staggering
with anything but radiance —
strike with the whole sky
over mother and father
and Crosshouse Road

strike me with untouched
centuries of cornflowers
if I'm running like an old man
who cannot imagine laughing